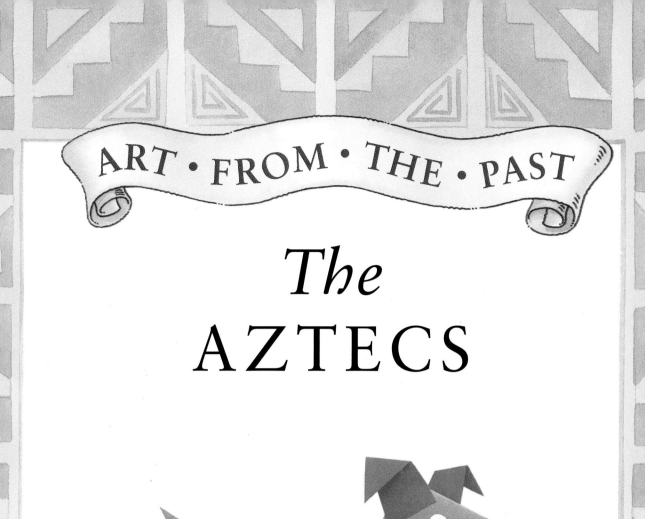

ART · FROM · THE · PAST

The
AZTECS

GILLIAN CHAPMAN

Heinemann

GENERAL CRAFT TIPS AND SAFETY PRECAUTIONS

Read the instructions carefully first, then collect together everything you need
before you start work.

It helps to plan your design out first on rough paper.

If you are working with papier mâché or paint, cover the
work surfaces with newspaper.

Always use a cutting mat when cutting with a craft knife and ask
an adult to help if you are using sharp tools.

Keep paint and glue brushes separate and always wash them out after use.
Use non-toxic paints and glue.

Don't be impatient – make sure plaster is set, and papier mâché and paint
are thoroughly dry before moving on to the next stage!

All projects make perfect presents!
Try to make them as carefully as you can.

RECYCLING

Start collecting materials for craftwork. Save newspaper, clean coloured
paper and card, cardboard boxes and tubes of different sizes, glossy paper
and gift wrap, and scraps of string and ribbon.

Clean plastic containers and old utensils are perfect for mixing
plaster and making paper pulp.

PICTURE CREDITS

Bodleian Library: 8 top, and 24; **British Museum:** 18; **Michael Holford:** 30; **Museum fur Volkerkunde:** 22;
Odyssey Productions: 20; **Reed Educational & Professional Publishing:** 14; **The Saint Louis Art Museum:**
28; **N.J. Saunders:** 6 top and bottom; **South American Pictures:** 34 © Tony Morrison; **Werner Forman Archive:**
7 top, 7 bottom © Museum fur Volkerkunde, 8 middle, 32 and 36 © National Museum of Anthropology, Mexico City,
8 bottom, 10 and 16 © British Museum, 26 © Pigorini Museum of Prehistory and Ethnography, Rome

ART FROM THE PAST: THE AZTECS was produced by
Fernleigh Books, 61A Southbury Road, Enfield, Middlesex, EN1 1PJ.

Designer: Gail Rose Photographer: Rupert Horrox
Illustrator: Teri Gower Picture Researcher: Jennie Karrach

First published in Great Britain in 1998 by Heinemann Library,
an imprint of Heinemann Educational Publishers,
Halley Court, Jordan Hill, Oxford OX2 8EJ,
a division of Reed Educational and Professional Publishing Ltd.

Heinemann is a registered trademark of Reed Educational
& Professional Publishing Limited.

OXFORD PORTSMOUTH NH (USA) CHICAGO
BLANTYRE MELBOURNE AUCKLAND
IBADAN GABORONE JOHANNESBURG

© Fernleigh Books 1998

British Library Cataloguing in Publication Data
Chapman, Gillian
The Aztecs. - (Art from the past)
1.Children - Craft - Juvenile literature 2.Handicraft -
Juvenile literature
I.Title 709.7′2

ISBN 0 431 08063 1

The author and Fernleigh Books would like to thank Martin Simpson, the
Fossil Man, for the loan of polished stone chips.

Printed in Italy.

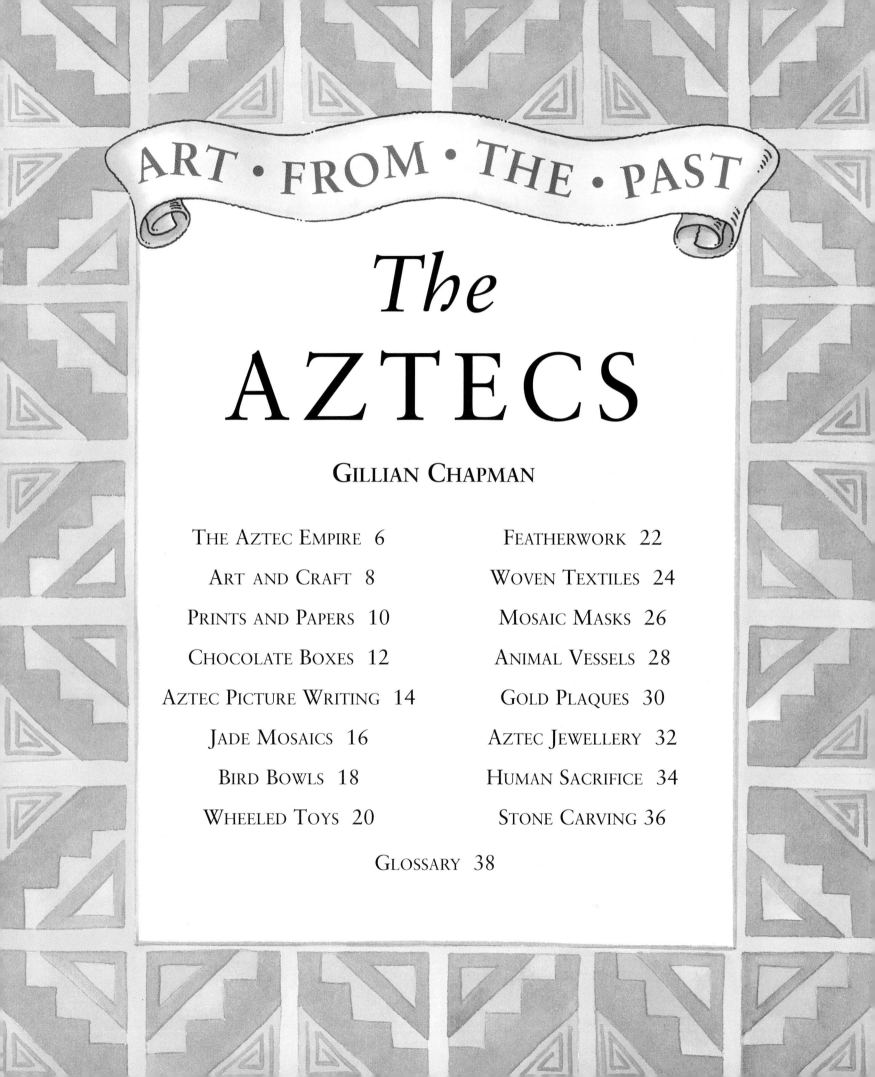

ART · FROM · THE · PAST

The AZTECS

Gillian Chapman

THE AZTEC EMPIRE

THE AZTECS were originally a small nomadic tribe who first settled in the Valley of Mexico in early 1300. Gradually they began to prosper and eventually conquered much of the surrounding areas, taking over land from neighbouring tribes.

At its peak the Aztec Empire contained over 15 million people, living in 500 towns and cities. Some of these cities were larger than European cities of the time. When the Spanish first arrived, the empire stretched across Mexico from the Atlantic to the Pacific.

The Aztecs were a tough race. They lived in a hot, barren land and were constantly at war. They believed in powerful gods that had to be kept content with human sacrifice. Otherwise the gods would become angry and destroy their world with earthquakes and drought.

Prisoners were taken from conquered cities, together with tribute that was paid to the Aztecs to prevent further attack. This system kept the Aztecs rich and supplied them with victims. At the time of the Spanish invasion they were sacrificing over 20,000 people a year.

TOP. *Stone walls in the Oaxaca Valley decorated with Aztec step designs.*

ABOVE. *Serpent head carved from stone.*

6

SUPERSTITION AND PROPHECY

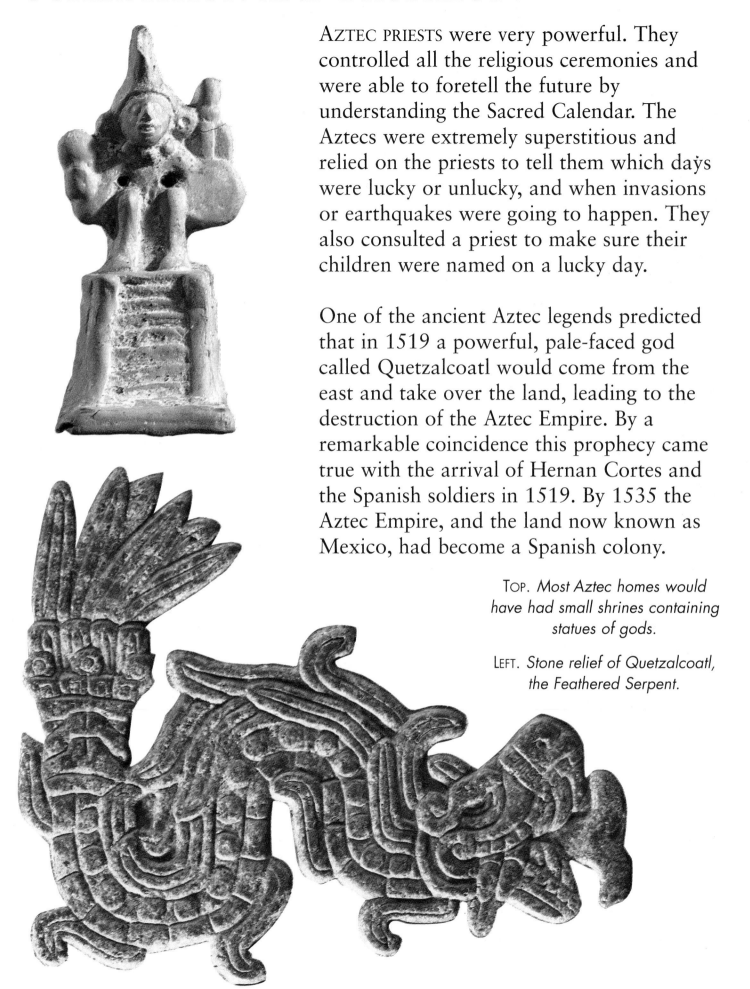

AZTEC PRIESTS were very powerful. They controlled all the religious ceremonies and were able to foretell the future by understanding the Sacred Calendar. The Aztecs were extremely superstitious and relied on the priests to tell them which days were lucky or unlucky, and when invasions or earthquakes were going to happen. They also consulted a priest to make sure their children were named on a lucky day.

One of the ancient Aztec legends predicted that in 1519 a powerful, pale-faced god called Quetzalcoatl would come from the east and take over the land, leading to the destruction of the Aztec Empire. By a remarkable coincidence this prophecy came true with the arrival of Hernan Cortes and the Spanish soldiers in 1519. By 1535 the Aztec Empire, and the land now known as Mexico, had become a Spanish colony.

TOP. *Most Aztec homes would have had small shrines containing statues of gods.*

LEFT. *Stone relief of Quetzalcoatl, the Feathered Serpent.*

ART AND CRAFT

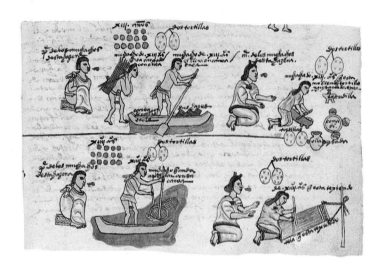

AZTEC PEASANTS made everything they needed from the natural materials they found. Clay was moulded into pots and baked in the sun. Reeds were woven into baskets and cactus fibres were spun into thread to make cloth, fishing nets and rope. They also brought goods into the city markets to trade.

As the empire grew the Aztecs traded with different tribes and discovered new materials and skills. They also took over large areas of land and the arts and crafts of the conquered peoples all became part of the Aztec style.

Large quantities of tribute was paid to the Aztecs in gold, feathers, animal skins, and anything of value. Tribute also included crafted items of woven cloth, jewellery, and pottery. Aztec craftworkers were influenced by the patterns and designs that came from other cultures.

Craftworkers were organised into guilds, with the skills and trade secrets of particular crafts passed down from father to son. Whole families worked together to make a particular item, like a feather shield (see page 22) or decorated cloak for a warrior.

TOP. *Drawings from a codex page show scenes of daily life.*

FAR RIGHT. *A gold earring made by Mixtec craftsmen.*

8

RIGHT. *Wooden drum decorated with owl carving.*

AZTEC CRAFT TIPS

There are many similarities between these projects and the craft techniques used by the Aztecs. Before starting a project look carefully at the Aztec crafts and try to use the colours and designs that they did.

To decorate some Aztec projects it is simple to make a design from scraps of coloured paper glued onto the surface, rather than to use paint. Coloured stickers or glued decorations make very colourful patterns.

If you are using materials, such as a pack of feathers, to decorate a project – sort them out first into piles of different colours. Try to use all the colours you have to best effect in your design.

Simple materials, such as coloured paper and gift wrap, can be used to decorate the Aztec projects.

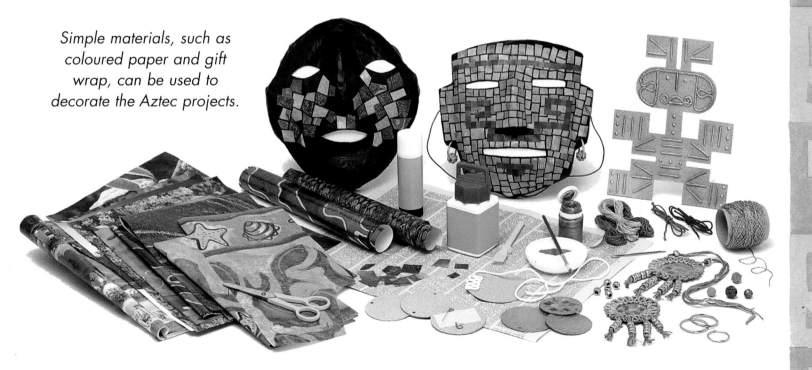

With the mosaic projects, use coloured pages from glossy magazines or scraps of gift wrap to make the mosaic pieces. Choose papers to give you the correct range of colours – blues, greens and turquoise.

To decorate projects with coloured papers and mosaic pieces plan your design first by arranging the pieces on the surface. When you are happy with the design, glue the pieces into position using a glue stick.

PVA glue is very useful for gluing card, string and collage materials like those used to make the Gold Plaques and the Aztec jewellery. It can be diluted with water to make papier mâché and paper pulp.

PRINTS AND PAPERS

THE AZTECS decorated their textiles and metalwork with distinctive patterns. Bands of repeating geometric designs and stylized animal shapes were painted or carved onto their pottery. Abstract patterns of zig-zag and stepped lines were most typical, usually painted in two colours.

Small carved relief blocks made from clay were used to stamp patterns onto fabric. This type of stamp was also used to paint the faces of dancers at festival time.

Aztec patterns are basically very simple. It is the way the designs are repeated in rows that makes them so effective and perfect for print designs.

DESIGNING PATTERNS

YOU WILL NEED
Scrap paper   Thick paints
Felt pens & pencil   Brush or roller
Newspaper   Paint tray
Craft knife   Paper & card
Printing block — Potato, soft eraser or polystyrene
Ask an adult to help you cut out the printing block.

1. Look at the Aztec patterns on this page and pages 6–7. Sketch some designs of your own on scrap paper, using one or two colours.

2. Keep your ideas simple and design them within a square or rectangular framework. Colour them in different ways to see which colours work best.

3. Either copy your design three or four times and see how it looks when repeated in a row, or if you can, photocopy it.

MAKING PRINTS

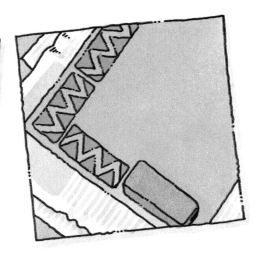

1. Simple designs are the most effective. Cut a potato in half. Draw the pattern on the surface of one half and cut it out carefully with a craft knife. Ask an adult to help you.

2. Small blocks of polystyrene packing or soft erasers also make good printing blocks. Draw the design on the flat surface and carefully cut it out with a craft knife.

3. Cover the work surface with newspaper. Dip the printing block into paint (alternatively brush or roller over the printing surface), then press it firmly onto the paper.

Use the printing blocks to decorate your own Aztec cards, wrapping paper, tags and bookmarks.

Printing designs onto a contrasting coloured paper can be very effective.

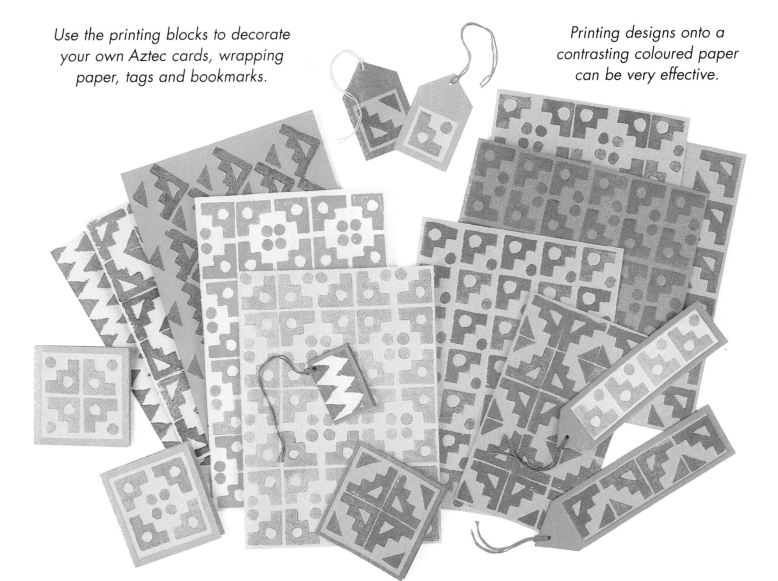

CHOCOLATE BOXES

AZTEC WORKERS and farmers lived on a very simple diet of maize, vegetables and fruit. The maize was ground into corn to make 'tortillas', flat pancakes, eaten at every meal. Wealthier people ate exotic foods like spices, pineapples and seafoods, which were all brought into the cities from warmer climates.

Today chocolate is still a luxury, although we can all afford to buy it. Try making some special Aztec gift boxes to put chocolates in. Stacked together they look like an Aztec temple! Aztecs held festivals at stepped temples like the one in the photograph above.

Rich and noble families also enjoyed a type of chocolate 'milkshake' made from ground cocoa beans mixed with water. The frothy mixture was sweetened with honey and vanilla.

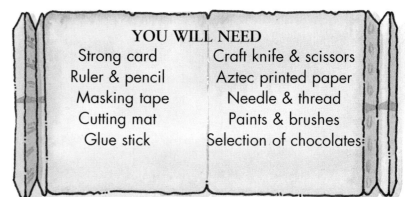

YOU WILL NEED

Strong card	Craft knife & scissors
Ruler & pencil	Aztec printed paper
Masking tape	Needle & thread
Cutting mat	Paints & brushes
Glue stick	Selection of chocolates

AZTEC BOX

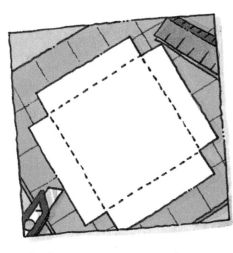

1. Draw a square in the centre of the strong card. This will be the base of the box. Then draw in the sides. Cut the outside of the shape out carefully.

2. Score along the four sides using the scissors and fold them up. Secure the sides with pieces of masking tape to form a box.

3. Cut out a square piece of card, 4 mm larger than the base, and tape it to one edge. Paint the box inside and out and leave to dry.

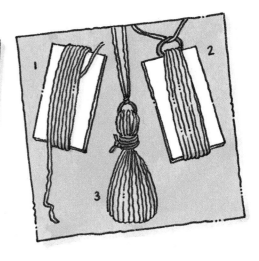

4. Make some printed paper with an Aztec design (see pages 10–11). Cut a printed strip the same depth as the box and stick it around the outside of the box using the glue stick.

5. Cut a printed square the same size as the lid and glue it on the lid. Make a tassel, thread it through the lid and secure it with tape. Cover the inside of the lid with a square of printed paper.

TASSEL MAKING

1. Wind a long length of thread around a piece of card.
2. Tie the threads together at the top and remove the card.
3. Wind some thread around the tassel, secure it with a knot, then cut through the ends.

Make a set of Aztec boxes – all different sizes.

Cover a plain box of chocolates with Aztec paper to make it extra special!

AZTEC PICTURE WRITING

THE AZTECS developed a very complex system of picture writing. Each picture, or 'glyph', represented an object or idea. Groups of glyphs made a larger picture story. It was a sophisticated system that only scribes and priests could interpret.

The Aztecs kept records of every aspect of their lives – payment of tribute, conquests in war, and domestic details. They believed in prophecies and avoided the unlucky days on their calendars.

They recorded information in large zig-zag books, called 'codices', made from bark paper or animal skin.

ZIG-ZAG CODEX

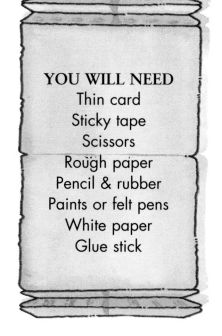

1. Tape the first two pages together, leaving a 1 cm gap between them. Neatly fold over the ends of the tape.

2. Cover the gap with a length of tape. Add pages until the codex is the right length for your story.

YOU WILL NEED
Thin card
Sticky tape
Scissors
Rough paper
Pencil & rubber
Paints or felt pens
White paper
Glue stick

PICTURE STORY

1. Aztec glyphs are very similar to cartoon strips. The story can be understood by looking at the pictures. Make up a short story and tell it as a series of glyphs.

2. Work out the story first on rough paper. You may prefer to draw the pictures on paper, colour them in, and then stick them into the codex.

3. The Aztecs showed speech as a tongue symbol coming out of a mouth, like a small speech bubble. A line of footprints indicated a journey.

This picture story tells the adventures of a group of friends on holiday together.

The Aztecs used glyphs to represent names, dates and ideas. Try thinking up glyphs to make your story really interesting!

15

JADE MOSAICS

YOU WILL NEED
Modelling clay
Newspaper
PVA glue & brush
Magazine pictures –
blue, turquoise,
green & orange
Scissors
Craft knife
Black paint & brush
Scraps of white card
Pipe cleaners

THE AZTECS loved precious stones and crafted them into magnificent statues, jewellery, masks and sacrificial objects. Green stones, like jade, turquoise and malachite, were particularly valued. Jade was the most precious as it symbolised water, the life-giving force.

Carved wooden shapes like this serpent were covered with pieces of stone or shell. Ceremonial death masks were made from a real skull, complete with teeth, and decorated with turquoise and shell mosaics.

TURQUOISE SERPENT

1. Take the clay and roll it into a long sausage shape. Use it to make the serpent's body. Then mould two heads and attach them to both ends.

2. Use a diluted PVA glue to cover the clay mould with six layers of newspaper strips. Use small paper pieces to cover the curves and corners. Leave to dry.

3. Remove the clay. Trim the edge of the shape with scissors. Carefully cut out the eye holes with a craft knife. Then paint the serpent black.

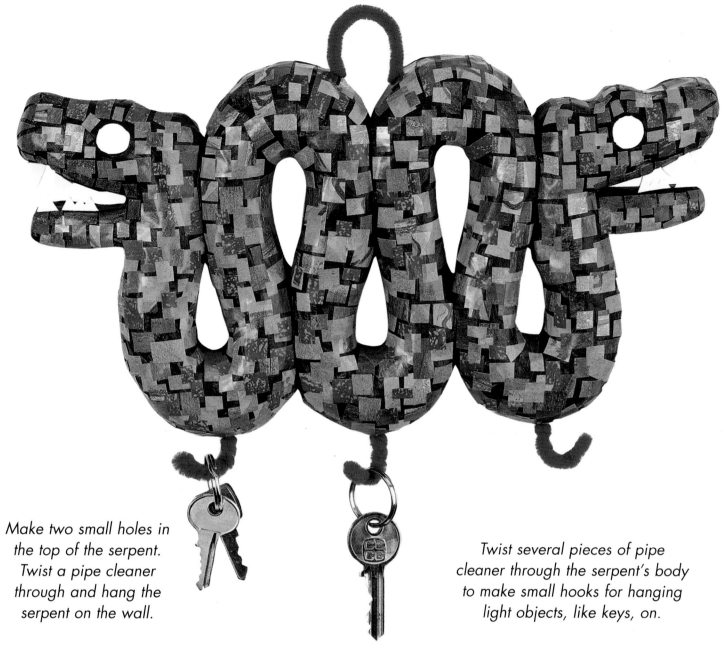

Make two small holes in the top of the serpent. Twist a pipe cleaner through and hang the serpent on the wall.

Twist several pieces of pipe cleaner through the serpent's body to make small hooks for hanging light objects, like keys, on.

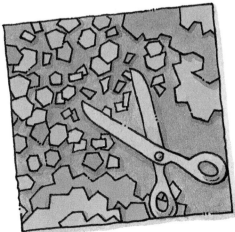

4. Cut up the turquoise, blue and green pictures into small pieces. The more shades of blue you can find, the better the finished mosaic will be.

5. Glue the pieces to the serpent. Look carefully at the photograph of the Aztec serpent and see how they used mosaic pieces of different sizes to great effect.

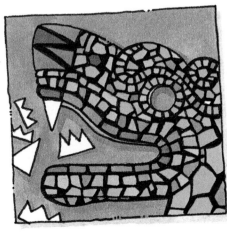

6. Complete the design by adding the nose and mouth details in orange pieces. Cut out teeth shapes from white card and glue them in place.

BIRD BOWLS

AZTEC POTTERY was shaped by hand, without using a potter's wheel. Some pots have carved animal forms, others are painted with detailed scenes from Aztec legends. Some are decorated inside and out with abstract patterns and designs (see page 10).

The Aztecs left no written records so much can be learnt about their history and culture from the picture stories painted on their pottery.

YOU WILL NEED

Newspaper	Modelling clay
Large & small bowl	Craft knife
with similar size bases	Scissors
PVA glue & brush	White emulsion paint
Cooking oil	Poster paints & brush
Cling film	Clear varnish & brush

BIRD BOWLS

1. Smear the inside and rims of both bowls with cooking oil and completely cover with cling film. Use a diluted PVA glue and cover the bowls with six layers of newspaper strips.

2. Make a bird shape from modelling clay and cover it with several layers of small newspaper strips. Then leave the bowls and bird shape to dry for at least two days.

3. When dry, the papier mâché shapes should come away easily from the bowls. Remove the cling film and trim the edges. Paste two layers of small strips over the trimmed edges and leave to dry.

The cup was made in the same way as the bowl. It has a parrot shaped handle and wooden beads sewn through the rim.

4. Carefully cut the paper bird shape in half with a craft knife and remove the modelling clay. Then glue the two halves together with small strips of paper.

5. Join the bowls together with PVA. Neaten the join by pasting strips of paper across. Stick the bird to the rim of the bowl with glued strips of paper.

6. Paint the bird bowl with two coats of white paint, allowing each coat to dry. Then paint on an Aztec design. Finally, varnish the bowl to protect it.

19

WHEELED TOYS

THE AZTECS did not realise that the wheel was very useful. They had no wheeled carts or wagons for transporting heavy loads and they shaped all their pottery without a potter's wheel. But they made wheeled animals to amuse their children!

Animals played a part in domestic life and religious rituals. Dogs were trained for hunting and some were bred for meat. Wild cats, like the jaguar, were worshipped for their power and strength.

Wheeled animals, like the carved toy dog shown in the photograph above, have been found in Aztec graves. The Aztecs believed that a wheeled dog would guide its master's soul to a final resting place.

WHEELED DOG

YOU WILL NEED

Stiff card	Two 15 cm lengths
Sharp pencil	of dowel
Scissors	Paints & brush
Four drawing pins	PVA glue & brush
Four plastic lids,	Ask an adult to help
the same size	you make the wheels.

1. Fold the card in half. Draw a simple animal shape on the card in pencil. Cut out the shape, cutting through both thicknesses of card, but not along the fold.

2. Mark the position of the wheel holes on the folded shape. Carefully pierce through the card using a sharp pencil. Make sure each pair of holes lines up.

3. Fold a small piece of card and draw the shape of an animal head onto it. Cut the animal head shape out and glue it to the body shape using PVA glue.

4. Decorate the folded shape to make it look like an animal. Aztec pottery and toy animals have stylized markings. Look at the designs on this page and pages 8–11. You may like to use one of the patterns on your animal.

5. Glue decorated circles of card onto the four lids and leave to dry. Carefully make a small hole in the centre of each lid by pushing a drawing pin through each one. You may need an adult's help with this.

6. Attach one lid to a length of dowel with a drawing pin. Thread the dowel through the holes, then pin another lid to the other end. Repeat for the second wheel axle. Make sure the dowel lengths both turn freely in the holes.

Glue extra features, such as card ears and a tail, to the animals for a finishing touch.

Make a collar and lead so your animal can guide you along!

FEATHERWORK

FEATHERWORK was a highly skilled craft. Spectacular clothing, such as capes and head-dresses, were made for emperors and high priests. Warriors wore feathered tunics and helmets – the higher the rank, the more elaborate the decoration. They carried leather shields (left) patterned with feather designs.

Tropical birds were hunted for their coloured feathers, but they were also bred in huge aviaries. Quetzal birds were prized for their beautiful plumage.

The Aztecs drew their designs onto cloth, then glued or sewed on feathers. Try making these feather mosaics on a shield or fan using the same Aztec techniques.

FEATHER SHIELD

YOU WILL NEED

Large & small circles of strong card	Pack of coloured craft feathers
Strips of strong card	Coloured card scraps
Sticky tape	
PVA glue & brush	Paper & pencil
Scissors	Stick handles

1. Draw the shield design on paper, then transfer it to the circle of strong card. Sort the craft feathers into piles of different colours.

2. Start on the outer edge of the shield and work in towards the centre. Glue a small area of the card and begin to cover it with feathers.

3. Following your design, overlap the feathers in layers, until the card is completely covered. Use the colours to the best effect in the design.

4. Make a circle pattern from the scraps of coloured card. Glue it to the shield to complete the design.

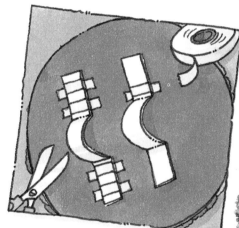

5. Finally tape strips of card to the back of the shield. Use these as grips for holding the shield.

The feather fans are made in the same way as the shield, only use smaller circles of card.

Decorate a small stick and tape it to the back of the fan to use as a handle.

WOVEN TEXTILES

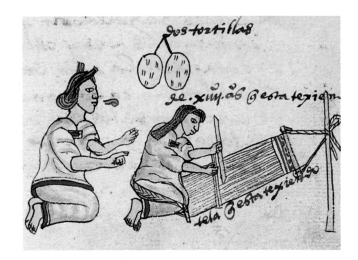

TEXTILES were extremely important in Aztec society. Vast quantities of textiles were offered to the gods and rich hangings decorated temples and were worn for religious processions.

The Aztecs did not keep sheep. Instead, they spun and dyed cotton and plant fibres. They then wove them into fabric using a 'back-strap' loom. People wore clothing that reflected their social class, but merchants wore plain cloaks of cactus fibre to hide their wealthy status.

Aztec girls learnt to weave at home. The picture above, taken from an Aztec codex, shows a mother teaching her daughter to weave. Aztec clothes were loose, simple and had no pockets so people probably carried small bags similar to the one on the far right. Why not weave your own bag!

YOU WILL NEED
Stiff card
Scissors
Long blunt needle
Coloured yarns
Felt for lining the bag

WOVEN BAG

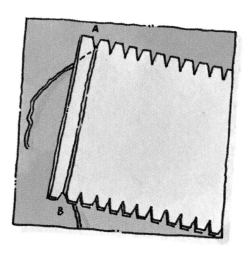

1. Remember the finished bag will be the same size as the card! Cut the same number of notches, 15 mm apart, from the top and bottom of the card.

2. Wind a length of strong yarn around the notches as shown. Secure the yarn into notch A, then wind it around the card into notch B.

3. Wind the yarn back into notch A, and then across into notch C. Then wind the yarn behind the card to notch D and take the yarn back to notch C.

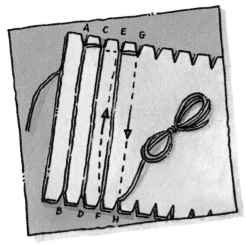

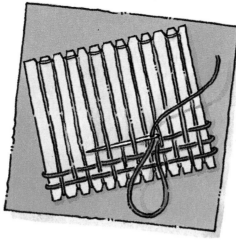

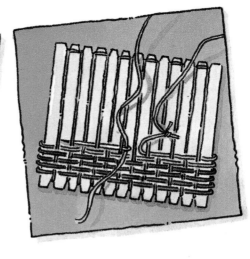

4. Take the yarn behind the card into E and down to F. From here, the yarn goes back to E, across into G and down to H. Continue following this sequence around all the notches. Secure both ends.

5. Thread a needle with a long length of yarn and weave it though the threads, in and out across the front, then across the back. Continue in this way, weaving around the card.

6. Tie on new lengths of yarn as needed and continue weaving lengths around the card until it is completely covered. Use lots of different colours to make a bright bag.

7. Secure the ends of the yarn. Carefully slip the loops over the top notches of the card, loosen the weaving from the bottom notches, then gently slide the card out.

Give the bag a plaited handle and decorate it with coloured tassels (see page 13). Line it with some coloured felt.

MOSAIC MASKS

MASKS played an important role in all Aztec festivals. Large stone masks were too heavy to be worn, but were used as temple decorations. During religious ceremonies they were made to represent the gods, attached to wooden frames and draped in elaborate costumes.

Burial masks often have very realistic portraits of Aztec faces. They were sculpted from special pieces of greenstone or granite, with eyes and teeth inlaid in shell. But the most spectacular Aztec masks were made with mosaics.

Craftworkers skilfully covered wooden masks, or even skulls, with tiny pieces of turquoise, jade and precious stones.

YOU WILL NEED

Paper & felt pens	PVA glue & brush
Ruler	Magazine pictures
Modelling clay	for mosaic work
Board	Scissors
Newspaper	Thin black elastic
Craft knife	Black paint & brush

MOSAIC MASK

1. First you will need to make a life-size sketch of a mask on paper. Either copy the ideas shown here or create your own design.

2. Take the modelling clay and place it on a board. Follow your design and roughly mould the clay into the mask shape, checking the size with a ruler.

3. When the mask is the right size, add more clay to build up the features, such as the forehead, cheeks and nose. Keep the clay surface smooth.

  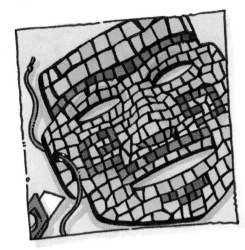

4. Use a diluted PVA glue to cover the mould with six layers of newspaper strips. Try to apply the paper evenly using small pieces to cover all the curves and corners.

5. When the mask is dry, carefully remove all the clay. Trim around the edge of the mask with scissors and cut out the eyes and mouth with a craft knife.

6. Paint the mask black. Cut the magazine pictures into pieces and use to make the mosaic pattern. Decorate the mask using the mosaic techniques on page 17.

Make holes in the mask and thread elastic through so you can either wear the mask or hang it on the wall.

Aztec masks were decorated with nose or ear ornaments and tufts of real hair! You could recreate this using fake fur!

ANIMAL VESSELS

THE FINEST and most decorative Aztec pottery was used exclusively by the rich or by priests during special rituals. Pots used everyday were very plain and simple, but all plates and bowls were shaped by hand.

Potters also made some very unusual vessels in the shape of birds and animals, such as dogs. The Aztecs kept dogs as pets and companions and believed they would guide them through the after-life.

Dog bones are commonly found in Aztec graves. They were probably buried next to their masters, along with dog shaped vessels, like the one above.

DOG VESSEL

YOU WILL NEED

Newspaper
Two large bowls
Hot water
(*Pulp will need to soak over night)

Clean empty container, card drum or tin
PVA glue & brush
Poster paint & brush
Clear varnish

1. To make the paper pulp, tear up newspaper into small pieces and put them in a large bowl. Cover the paper pieces with hot water and leave them to soak over night.

2. Take handfuls of paper, squeeze out all the water and place it in the second bowl. Then mash it together with PVA glue, using your hands, until it feels soft and smooth.

3. Press small lumps of pulp to the sides of the container and work all the way round, building up the animal shape. Brush on extra PVA to help the pulp stick to the sides.

Try making an unusual vessel in the shape of your favourite animal and use it to keep your desk tidy.

4. Pulp is very easy to model with your fingers. Make the large body and head shapes first by pressing the pulp firmly together. Add more pulp to make the ears, paws and tail.

5. Gently rub over the surface with your fingers to make it smooth and remove any lumps. Then put the dog vessel in a safe place and leave it to thoroughly dry out.

6. Paint the container inside and out and leave to dry. Either use natural clay colours or bright jazzy patterns. Then apply two coats of clear varnish to protect it.

GOLD PLAQUES

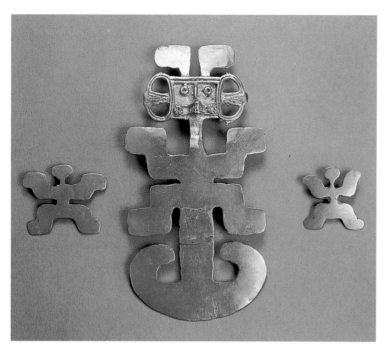

THE AZTECS were famous for their gold jewellery and metal-work, but few pieces survive today. Much was taken back to Spain by the Conquistadors and melted down to make gold bars. Aztec goldsmiths were very skilled and held high status in society. They produced elaborate jewellery, lip and nose plugs, masks and pendants, as well as golden temple decorations.

The golden plaque designs on this page are based on these stylised Tolima figures (above) made from beaten gold. Make an Aztec gold plaque to hang on the wall.

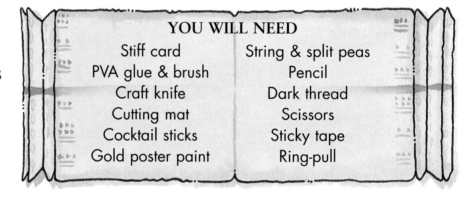

YOU WILL NEED

Stiff card	String & split peas
PVA glue & brush	Pencil
Craft knife	Dark thread
Cutting mat	Scissors
Cocktail sticks	Sticky tape
Gold poster paint	Ring-pull

GOLDEN PLAQUE

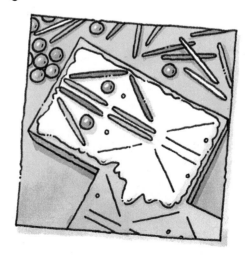

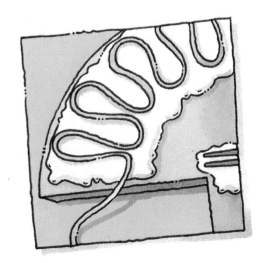

1. Copy the plaque outline on to the card and draw in the pattern detail. Use the craft knife to cut out the card shape.

2. Spread a thin layer of glue over part of the card. Follow the design and glue pieces of stick, string and split peas to the card.

3. Continue to build up the raised pattern over the whole plaque, making sure all the pieces are stuck down firmly.

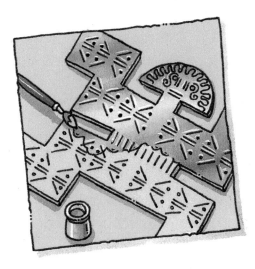

4. Leave somewhere safe and let the glue dry. When the glue is dry, paint the plaque with gold poster paint.

5. Cut out four circles of card and paint them gold. Hang them from the head with pieces of thread, taped to the back.

6. Glue a ring-pull to the back of the plaque and use it to hang the plaque on the wall.

Make these colourful plaques of Aztec gold to hang on the wall.

To make the gold plaque look really old, dab it with bronze paint.

AZTEC JEWELLERY

When the Spanish Conquistadors entered Tenochtitlan in 1519, they were amazed at the wealth of the Aztecs. The Emperor Montezuma believed, through a prophecy, that the Spanish leader was a god. He showered Cortes with gifts of gold and beautiful jewellery.

The Spanish became greedy and in the conflict that followed, they plundered all the Aztecs' treasure. It was taken back to Spain, where all the spectacular gold jewellery and decorations were melted down.

A few pieces survived, like this turquoise and gold brooch. Try and re-create some Aztec jewellery using these mosaic designs.

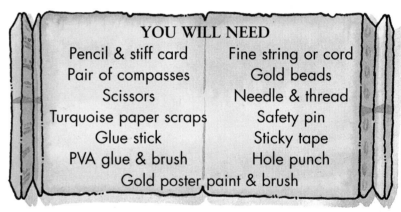

YOU WILL NEED

Pencil & stiff card	Fine string or cord
Pair of compasses	Gold beads
Scissors	Needle & thread
Turquoise paper scraps	Safety pin
Glue stick	Sticky tape
PVA glue & brush	Hole punch
Gold poster paint & brush	

MOSAIC MEDALLIONS

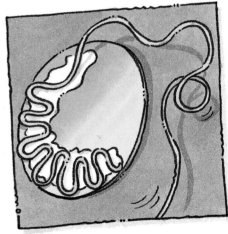

1. To make the simple medallion shape, draw a circle on the card with the compasses. Carefully cut out the circle with scissors and paint it gold.

2. Cut the turquoise paper scraps into small pieces. Arrange these on the gold circle to make the mosaic design, then stick them in place with the glue stick.

3. To make a more detailed medallion, first glue a length of curled string around the edge of the circle using PVA. Paint it gold and complete the mosaic in the centre.

PENDANTS AND BROOCHES

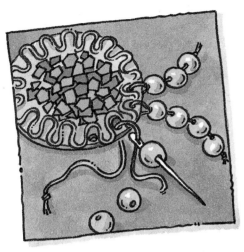

1. Punch four small holes along the bottom edge of a medallion and attach strings of gold beads. Tape a safety pin to the back of the card to make a brooch.

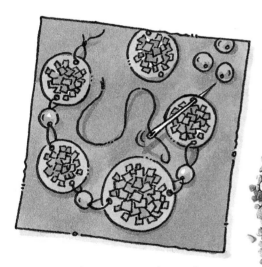

2. Try making a number of medallions of different sizes and designs. The pendant and necklace are made by making holes in several medallions and threading them together with the gold beads.

The mosaic pendant shown here recreates the Aztec brooch design opposite.

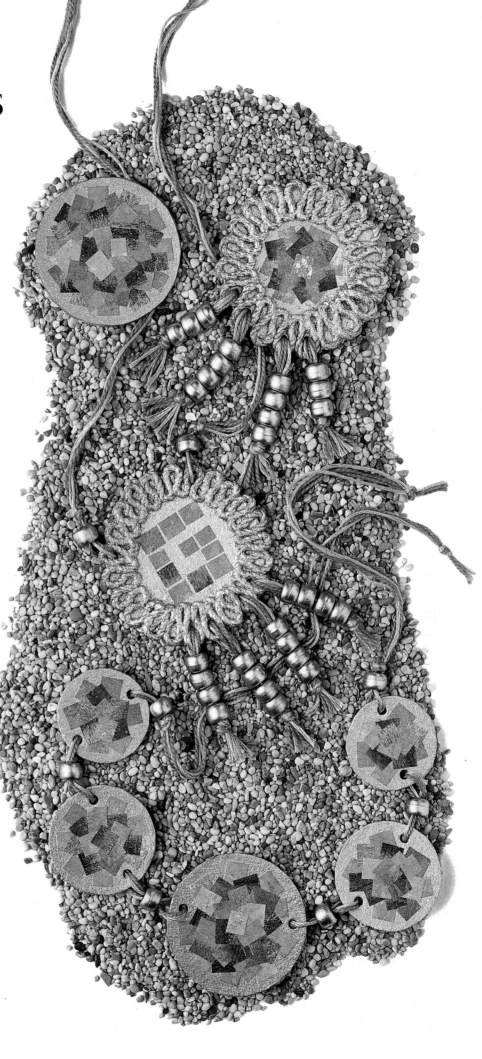

HUMAN SACRIFICE

THE AZTECS worshipped many gods and human sacrifice was an important part of their religion. They believed offerings of hearts and blood pleased the gods and kept the sun alive. Sacrifices were held in the Great Temple, which looked like a huge stepped pyramid (see page 12).

During important festivals hundreds of slaves and prisoners were killed. Priests cut out their hearts with sacrificial knives and threw the bodies down the blood-stained temple steps.

In the Temple, reclining stone statues, called chacmools, represented the messenger of the gods. Sacrificial hearts were placed in their laps.

CHACMOOL BOOKENDS

YOU WILL NEED

Pairs of boxes (see Step 1)	Paints & brush
	Coloured paper scraps
PVA glue & brush	Pencil & felt pens
Sand or small stones (to weigh the bookends)	Scissors
	Glue stick
Sticky tape	Pairs of plastic lids

1. To make one bookend you will need two boxes, one twice as long as the other, but both of similar widths. They will be glued together to make the bookend shape.

2. Fill the larger box with sand or gravel, and seal it closed with plenty of tape. Tape up the smaller box and glue them both together using PVA glue.

3. Repeat this process with the other boxes, so you have two bookend shapes. Paint the boxes to cover up the strips of tape and any printing on the surfaces.

This pair of Chacmools are not so gruesome! They are great fun to make and are perfect bookends.

The lids on their laps make handy containers for paper clips, coins or even the occasional chocolate heart.

4. Decorate the front of the bookends with coloured paper shapes. Carefully cut out a simple chacmool figure from paper and glue one to the front of each bookend.

5. To decorate the sides and top of each bookend, cut out some paper shapes and glue them together to make colourful patterns. Or colour the surfaces with felt pen designs.

6. Glue a plastic lid on the top of each chacmool using PVA – they make attractive hats! A second upturned lid glued to the body makes a handy desk tidy.

STONE CARVING

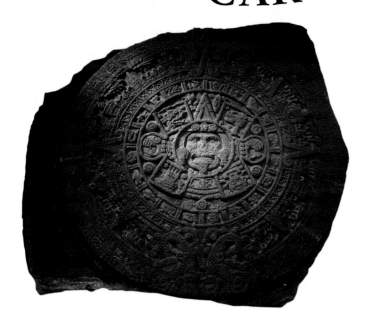

The largest known Aztec sculpture is a circular stone relief known as the Sun stone, or Calendar. The Aztecs were very superstitious and consulted the calendar to make horoscopes and prophecies.

THE AZTEC CITY of Tenochtitlan became the most powerful city in Mexico. It was home for 100,000 people, a great trading centre, and was well planned on a grid system of streets and causeways.

The Aztecs created the city with many practical amenities such as canals, aqueducts and reservoirs. They also built impressive stone buildings – palaces, temples and ball courts, which were richly decorated with carved stone friezes (see page 6). As religion and mythology were central to Aztec life, these carvings depicted the legends of the gods and would originally have been brightly painted. Try painting your Aztec tile in bright oranges, reds and yellows.

CARVED TILE

1. Draw a design for the tile on tracing paper. Keep your ideas simple and try copying a figure or pattern from the Aztec carving shown above.

2. Measure the design and make a cardboard mould the same size, with sides 5 cm deep. Turn up the sides and secure them with tape.

3. Following the instructions on the packet, mix up some plaster and pour it into the mould to a depth of 3 cm. Smooth the surface and leave to dry.

YOU WILL NEED

Tracing paper & pencil · Sticky tape
Strong cardboard · Paints & brush
Ruler · Newspapers
Cutting mat & craft knife · Nail or carving tool
Plaster, an old plastic container
& mixing utensils

4. Make sure the plaster is dry. Remove it from the mould. Choose the smooth side to work on and paint the surface with a thick coat of paint.

Try painting the tile in several different colours to give a more interesting finish, then leave to dry.

5. Trace your design onto the painted surface so an impression is left on the paint. Then carefully scratch out the line using a sharp nail or carving tool.

If you scratch out a line by mistake just paint it over with some paint of the same colour!

GLOSSARY

Abstract – design or pattern made from shapes with no recognisable forms.

Artefact – object or work of art made by craftworkers.

Back-strap loom – simple loom used to weave cloth; one end is fixed to a tree or post, with the other supported by a strap around the weaver's waist.

Ball courts – huge walled courtyards, over 100 metres long, decorated with stone carvings and statues, where ball games were played.

Bark paper – paper material used to make codices, made from the bark of the wild fig tree.

Causeway – raised pathway crossing a flooded area.

Chacmool – large reclining stone figure found in the temple, representing a messenger of the gods.

Sacrificial hearts and blood were placed in their laps as food for the gods.

Codex – zig-zag book, made from bark paper or parchment, illustrated with glyphs. Many codices contain information about Aztec conquests, records of tribute and details of daily life, religious beliefs and prophecies.

Conquistadors – Spanish explorers and soldiers who travelled to Tenochtitlan in the 16th century.

Cortes (Hernan) – the leader of the Spanish Conquistadors, who arrived in Tenochtitlan with Spanish soldiers in 1519.

Festivals – special days of celebration, usually a holiday when everyone would join in with the festivities.

Glyph – a picture sign making up the Aztec system of picture writing.

Guild – organisation, like a modern trade union, made up of workers of the same craft.

Mixtec – an early civilization living in what is now called Mexico around 1200 BC.

Montezuma – the Emperor who ruled the Aztec Empire at the time of the Spanish Conquest.

Mosaic – a work of art made from tiny pieces of precious stones or shell, carefully pieced together.

Nomadic – to wander with no fixed abode.

Prophecy – a story or legend that predicts what will happen in the future.

Quetzal – a tropical bird, highly prized by the Aztecs for its beautiful plumage and tail feathers.

Relief – a design which is raised above, or cut into, its background.

Ritual – a ceremony, with special prayers and actions, performed as an offering to the gods.

Sacrifice – an offering, sometimes animal or human, made to please the gods. The Aztecs believed that if the sacrifices stopped the world would come to an end.

Scribe – professional writer and record keeper, who could read and write the Aztec system of picture writing.

Superstitious – believing in good luck and bad omens.

Tenochtitlan – the name of the ancient Aztec capital city, known today as Mexico City.

Textiles – all cloth and fabric, either woven or non-woven, made from yarn or fibres

Tortillas – a flat pancake, made from ground maize kneaded into a dough and cooked – still eaten in Mexico today.

Tribute – the payment of valuable goods to the Aztecs by their conquered neighbours. If they stopped paying tribute it would lead to war.